POTENT WITHIN

POTENT WITHIN

Yinka Akintunde

RESOURCE HOUSE
LONDON

POTENT WITHIN
Copyright © Yinka Akintunde 2010

All Rights Reserved

ISBN 978-0-9568267-3-2

Published by
RESOURCE HOUSE
info@diademministries.org
resourcehouse@ymail.com
www.diademministries.org

All Bible quotations have been taken from the King James
Version of the Bible, unless otherwise indicated in the text.
'NKJV' refers to the New King James Version; 'NIV' refers to the
New International Version.

Printed for Resource House

Contents

Introduction

And God said 'Let us make man in our image, after our likeness: and let them have dominion over the fish of the sea, and over the fowl of the air, and over the cattle, and over all the earth, and over every creeping thing that creeps upon the earth.'

So God created man in his own image, in the image of God created he him; male and female created he them.

Genesis 1:26–27

The man created in God's image is not black or white, not Chinese, Japanese, Jewish or Hispanic. The man made in God's image is not fat or thin, he is neither tall nor short; the man made in God's image is a spirit. Man is not categorised according to skin colour, race, tribe or any of the terms used to describe man today. Man is in God's image and God is none of those mentioned above. God is neither Jew nor Greek; God is not black, white or in between; God is a spirit.

And the Lord God formed man of the dust of the ground, and breathed into his nostrils the breath of life; and man became a living soul.

Genesis 2:7

God formed a body for the man created in His image, so the man could take a form, an earth-compatible form. The form the real man took is what people naively use in describing man. The man is not the form (body), but the owner of the form. The dominant personality in the entity called man is not the form or the body, the dominant entity is the created man – a spirit man created in God's (spirit) image.

The Fall of Man in Eden killed the created man and left the form to roam the earth, until the fullness of the divine plan is fulfilled through Christ, so that real man can live again. Every man born of man's seed is a formed man, or has a form the real man puts on like a garment; God con-firmed this when talking of what happened in Jeremiah's mother's womb.

> *Then the word of the Lord came unto me, saying, 'Before I formed thee in the belly I knew thee; and before thou camest forth out of the womb I sanctified thee, and I ordained thee a prophet unto the nations.'*
>
> *Jeremiah 1:4–5*

This is why the physical form will look different from person to person, family to family, race to race and nation to nation. The form takes after the womb or lineage it is formed in, but the real man takes after God in whose image he was created.

Jesus came to redeem, restore and revive the real man. The man is then said to be born again, recreated in the similitude of Christ who is the image of God. The recreated or reborn man is spirit. Therefore, when you are born again, you are born of the spirit and so you are a spirit. You cannot be born of the spirit and yet be merely flesh with a soul, as like will only beget like.

When a man gets born again, he is not spiritual, he is a spirit, he ought to be spiritually minded, which means, though he lives in a body, his mind, which is part of his soul, tends towards the spirit. His mind agrees with and functions in the realm of the spirit, where his true personality lives. This is not the same as the 'spiritism' practised by followers of the occult, neither is it the pseudo-religion seen in falsely religious people, who hide their heads in the clouds, pretending to be spiritual and conforming to a norm or tradition that has no scriptural basis and does not contribute to one's spiritual development or proffer tangible solutions to life's issues based on the light of Scripture. A believer is essentially a spirit living in a body, possessing a soul. An unbeliever is essentially a body possessing a soul and a dead spirit. What a life!

If you are a spirit-man, you must know how to relate, while living physically on earth, with the realm of the spirit, for that is your true realm. You cannot do this with a bare mind and body.

Ye are seated with Christ in heavenly places.

Ephesians 2:6

The 'heavenly places' refers to the spirit realm where God, Christ and angelic beings dwell in light, which means there is a corollary to this realm, which is that of darkness, from where Satan and his demons operate.

You are not a man because you live in a body; man is man because God called him a man... *God said, 'Let us make man...'* (Genesis 1:26).

As a believer who is essentially a spirit, you should be as concerned and involved (if not more so) with the realm of the spirit as with the earthly realm. You therefore need your spirit to function properly. It is vital (living) and grows ever stronger through the limitless abilities of God, by redemption and the indwelling Holy Spirit, so it can function properly on earth. You need your spirit ability in order to relate properly to God and please Him. Jesus said those who will worship (relate to) God will do so in spirit and in truth or reality. The word 'worship' does not mean singing a slow song, but is an art of relating to the Supreme God in reverence, subjection and service.

You also need the proper functioning of your spirit in order to relate with the right perspective, and to obtain the right result in spite of and over the kingdom of darkness all the time and every time. You need this in order to put darkness where it belongs, which is beneath your feet. You need the proper functioning of your spirit to succeed on earth in your God-given assignment; you need it to be able to subdue your environment in your favour, no matter how unfavourable and hostile it initially seems.

When the spirit-man functions and relates properly to the spirit realm, the soul and the body have no choice but to follow suit. As a man, you were born into the world essentially as a body and soul with a dead spirit, you have thus learnt the way to live like that over a long period of time. When you are born again, you need to unlearn certain things; you also need to learn many new things. You must learn how to function properly in the realm of the spirit, how to properly harness and engage the ability of your spirit on daily basis. This is an integral part of the new things you must learn. You can't do this by mere intellect, physique or physical attributes.

Now this I say, brethren, that flesh and blood can-not inherit the kingdom of God; neither doth corruption inherit incorruption.

1 Corinthians 15:50

The man on earth needs to engage the man in the heavenly place because that is the true man made in the image of God. Among a few other things, this book is intended to help you appreciate this man of the spirit and engage him as an unconquerable, formidable force within you that cannot fail or falter. I then foresee your life becoming a sweet ride, as it was in Eden, and even sweeter, for *'better is the end of a thing than the beginning thereof'* (Ecclesiastes 7:8b).

Chapter One

The Ability of your Spirit

The eventual result of your Christian journey and your success in life's race will ultimately depend on how well you unlock the inherent abilities of the new man you come to recognise and how well you make use of what is available for you in Christ. The truth is, there is no short cut in the things of the spirit.

When the children of Israel left Egypt, they saw miracles, sang good songs and had dreams of finding fulfilment in their new-found freedom. But of about three million, only Caleb and Joshua made it in the congregation:

> *Moreover, brethren, I would not that ye should be ignorant, how that all our fathers were under the cloud, and all passed through the sea; and were all baptised unto Moses in the cloud and in the sea; and did all eat the same spiritual meat; and did all drink the same spiritual drink: for they drank of that spiritual Rock that followed them: and that Rock was Christ. But with many of them God*

was not well pleased: for they were overthrown in the wilderness.

1 Corinthians 10:1–5

But God said that Caleb had another spirit within him.

But as truly as I live, all the earth shall be filled with the glory of the Lord. Because all those men which have seen my glory, and my miracles, which I did in Egypt and in the wilderness, and have tempted me now these ten times, and have not hearkened to my voice; surely they shall not see the land which I sware unto their fathers, neither shall any of them that provoked me see it: But my servant Caleb, because he had another spirit with him, and hath followed me fully, him will I bring into the land where into he went; and his seed shall possess it.

Numbers 14:21–24

Caleb's engagement in the realm of the spirit, his positioning and attitude was different from the others, though they all looked alike, ate the same food and had same challenges at hand. God was not even interested in the degrees they obtained, their age, sex or skin colour. He was not interested in their church denomination or tribe; how close they were to the man of God, Moses, was irrelevant. It was a matter of their spirit, not their post or position in the assembly, not their title in the society, not how much gold or silver or cloth they had, it was their spirit. That was what determined their end and *'better is the end of a thing than the beginning thereof'* (Ecclesiastes 7:8b).

Nicodemus was astonished at the level of life, victories and results Jesus was commanding. He then went to Him and asked Him the secret of such a life. The question of Jesus's office as a teacher and a prophet did not arise; neither did he doubt the God whom Christ was serving, for he said, 'We know you are a teacher (office) sent from God.' They had seen similar office-holders before, and seen their intimidating ceremonial dress, but that was all there was to it. There was no life, no vitality, no victory; they feared what others feared, they fell for what others fell for, so Nicodemus was nominated to go and find out why and how. The answer Jesus gave was unexpected: he should have read them his résumé, told them all the schools he attended, told them how specially anointed he was and how much offering they needed give to tap into that. But no, the master did not do that; here is Jesus's response:

Question: How do you get these good results?
Answer: Except a man be born again, he cannot see the kingdom of God.

What a character Jesus was! 'We know you are the one saving people,' Nicodemus would have said, 'so you need no salvation or deliverance, but what has a man being born again got to do with this? We are talking about getting good results when we face life's issues, getting things done God's way, invincibility in the face of opposition and challenges. We are talking about undeniable divine presence manifesting in divine help, backing and response.'

Jesus then further said, 'A man has to be born of the spirit.'

Did you say 'born of the spirit'?

Jesus said 'Yes.' So that they would know He knew what he was talking about, he further said, 'That which is born of the spirit is spirit and such are they who can operate in the dimension of life you are asking about. The wind blow where it lists and you cannot stop it but you will see the impact of its engagement; such is he that is born of the spirit.'

Jesus answered, 'I tell you the truth, no one can enter the kingdom of God unless he is born of water and the Spirit. Flesh gives birth to flesh, but the Spirit gives birth to spirit. You should not be surprised at my saying, "You must be born again." The wind blows wherever it pleases. You hear its sound, but you cannot tell where it comes from or where it is going. So it is with everyone born of the Spirit.'

John 3:5–8 (NIV)

In a nutshell, Jesus was saying that the results we obtain in life depend on how much spirit-force a man is able to put into engagement, irrespective of the fact that we are all connected to God as his people. When a man is born again, Jesus said, it is like a blowing wind – you see the effect of the spirit life in man's earthly life; the force getting it done is not optically tangible, yet it does exist.

'The wind blows where it lists or pleases.' So it is not an accident or happenstance. A Christian cannot be lucky or fortunate in how much spirit-force he engages in the affairs of life. Nothing happens unless you make it happen; change has to be effected by someone. People who live on luck have no control over life's issues, so anything can happen to them – life or death, good or bad, no beginning, no ending.

God is a Spirit

God is not a spiritual being. His presence or essence is what creates a spiritual environment, no wonder He is called the *'Father of all spirits'* (Hebrews 12:9). Adam, created in the similitude of God, was a spirit living in a body made of dust. The true source of Adam's being was God's Word

('Let us make man') rendered as 'make man'. This was the spoken Word that brought the concept of mankind into existence. Jesus said these words were *'spirit'* (John 6:63). They were not spiritual words, they were spirit. The same concept was adopted when Jesus came into the world. To a casual eye, Jesus was born by Mary, but in actual fact Mary had no input, per se, in the birth of Jesus. She was just a vessel, like the earth from which God took the dust when He made Adam. What became Jesus the man in Mary's womb was not an ovum; if it were, there would need to have been a sperm cell, but none was needed.

Jesus was an absolute product of God's Word (John 1:1). The same Word gave birth to Adam; the Word was the spirit and life that Adam had. Adam's body, made of dust, was what he and Eve saw after falling, stripped of glory and naked. This was so because he had broken the Word (the spirit and the life) and thus he was dead. It was just a matter of time before the body would fall down and rot. The life Adam had, which was the life of God, was so powerful that it took Adam's body a very long time to drop dead, even after the main man was dead within. Adam lived nine hundred and thirty years with just his body (Genesis 5:1–3).

The influence of the law of sin and death, which came into existence immediately after the Fall, can be seen in people who lived after Adam as well. Adam switched it on by disobedience and it came into manifestation gradually. The world system is ruled by laws. The discovery of physical laws is what gave birth to science. The world and nature are governed by the law of sin and death as is everything natural.

People erroneously think the present human body was what Adam had in Eden. No, not at all. The present human body came out of a process of metamorphosis under the influence of the law of sin and death. In Eden, Adam could hear God with his natural ear and not be afraid or tremble. Years later, the children of Israel could not do so; even Moses himself was afraid. Adam could see God with his eyes; he could speak to the snake and hear it with his ears. Men since Adam cannot do these things.

After the Fall, the full degeneration of the earth and man's nature took some time. Think of Noah. He was a farmer, yet before the flood he needed no rain to grow his crops, for it never rained before then and there was no drought. He could control lions, crocodiles and other dangerous animals on the ark simply because they were not dangerous; they only metamorphosed into the wild bunch we have today under the progressive influence of the law of sin and death introduced by man's Fall. He probably sent for some of them miles from where he was living before he could put them on the ark.

Until God made people speak in tongues at Babel, all humanity spoke the same language. This unified language was obviously not English, Chinese, Japanese, Yoruba, Latin, Greek, German or Zulu. All languages today are post-Babel languages. Adam did not speak any of these; Adam spoke God's language and so did the people after him, until the great confusion of Babel. It was the introduction and festering of the law of sin and death which brought about all the differences between fallen man and pre-Fallen Adam, be-tween the Garden of Eden and the present world. This is why natural man, with his earthly knowledge, sees biblical accounts as too ridiculous to be real.

If God is a spirit, he therefore dwells in spirit realm. If God is a spirit, so is the devil. The angels are spirit and dwell in spirit realm, so are demons (Psalm 104:4). If God, the devil, angels and demons are spirit, then it would be unwise for a human, who is essentially a spirit living in a body, to be oblivious to the spirit world. The spirit world was the first world. God spoke the material world into existence from the realm of the spirit. The spirit world is the superior world; the decision to create the material world was made there ('come, let us'). God – a spirit – spoke this in the spirit world to spirit beings about His divine plan to create an existence in the earthly realm. The archetype of the material world was formed in the spirit world. God called the things that are not as if they exist (Romans 4:17), which means that the fact that they did not have material existence in the physical realm did not compromise the reality of their existence to God in spirit realm. The timing system of the material world was formed from the timeless spiritual world; what we call day and night today was spoken into existence by God from the spirit realm.

> *And God saw the light, that it was good: and God divided the light from the darkness. And God called the light Day, and the darkness he called Night. And the evening and the morning were the first day.*
>
> *Genesis 1:4–5*

The destinies of men are determined and orchestrated in the spirit world before they are manifested, pursued, fulfilled or missed in the earthly realm, as can be seen in the following situations:

- Babel: *'Let us go down and there confound their language, that they may not under-stand one another's speech.'* (Genesis 11:7).
- Nebuchadnezzar: *'Let his heart be changed from man's, and let a beast's heart be given*

unto him; and let seven times pass over him. This matter is by the decree of the watchers, and the demand by the word of the holy ones: to the intent that the living may know that the most High ruleth in the kingdom of men, and give it to whomsoever he will, and setteth up over it the basest of men.' (Daniel 4:16–17).

- Jeremiah: *'Then the word of the Lord came unto me, saying, "Before I formed thee in the belly I knew thee; and before thou camest forth out of the womb I sanctified thee, and I ordained thee a prophet unto the nations." '* (Jeremiah 1:4–5).

- Paul the Apostle: *'But when it pleased God, who separated me from my mother's womb, and called me by his grace.'* (Galatians 1:15).

A man's disposition to the spirit realm will eventually determine his position here on earth and much more in eternity. If God is a spirit, Adam, made in the likeness of God, must also be a spirit, so is every other human who came in the similitude of Adam. Adam lived in a body and had a soul, as do all humans. Man is not just a body mass or a collection of molecules. Not many will want to believe it; it sounds unscientific to them. I have heard many say, 'When you die, you rot and that is all.' They do not believe in the reality of the spirit-and-soul entity, to them such things are not real, and spiritual experience is just some form of hallucination or mishandled brain activity.

But let us consider these three scenarios in the Holy Bible:

(i)   Jesus told the thief, *'Today you will be with me in paradise'* (Luke 23:39–43).

But the man's body died, that is why he was crucified in the first place. Even if the sceptics argue that Jesus did not die, they will agree that the thief did die, for he had a death sentence on him. Jesus did not say 'You will meet me at the town centre or nearby village,' but 'paradise', where the justified go after death in the Old Testament. So Jesus died and so did the man, but they were to meet that day in paradise.

(ii) Saul, the backsliding King of Israel, asked the necromancers to help him raise Samuel for consultation. Samuel was dead, buried and his body rotten, but the necromancer agreed. The necromancer, whose spirit eyes were opened, saw Samuel appear as Saul used to know him. He also had a robe on him and he came up towards them. But the woman herself called the man approaching a spirit, for he had died years before and was buried, his body rotten, but the spirit-man still existed, awaiting the redemption of all things. The man Saul spoke with was Samuel's spirit, even though Samuel's body was dead. It was Samuel who spoke, not Saul's imagination. He recognised Saul; he spoke to him and even expressed his ill feeling at Saul's disturbance ('why are you disturbing me?'). He also prophesied. Saul was told by Samuel, 'Today you shall be with me', and that Israel's army would be defeated by the Philistines. Saul died that very day, beheaded, though he was not buried that day. So Samuel was not talking of his body. His body was burnt and his ashes were buried the following day. But his spirit, which Samuel referred to as 'you', went to be with the dead that same day (1 Samuel 28:8–19).

So the *you* in 'you' is a spirit, dead or alive; you are still essentially a spirit, even after you have been buried or cremated.

(iii) Jesus said, ***'What will it profit a man to gain the whole world and lose his soul?'*** (Mark 8:36).

The man in question here is not a soul (mind, will and emotion), because that is what this man is about to lose; if you lose a possession, you are not that possession. The soul is man's possession – no wonder that when people have a mental problem, they refer to them as losing their mind. The man in question has to die before losing his soul – dead in the sense of physical termination of the natural life, with the body disintegrated back into dust or ashes. If dying is the end of man's existence, as many believe, why count the loss again? But here we see Jesus lamenting how much of a loss the man will incur if, after the death of the body, the soul is lost to hell. That means the man will know how much he is losing. Now the body is dead, the soul is lost and he still refers to the man. It can only be the third entity in man's trilogy he is referring to – the spirit. So here we see Christ referring to the spirit of man as the man himself.

Chapter Two

Truly an Evolution

The man we know today is essentially an evolved man – this is not evolution in the sense of godless theory, as in Darwin's confused mind, but evolution in terms of change resulting from a shift in the spirit status of man and thus the operation of his soul and body. This is not evolution in the sense that man evolved from chimpanzees – let God be true and all men, evolution theorists included, be liars. The Word of God said that God created man in His image. *'In the similitude of divinity created he them male and female'* (Genesis 1:27).

The man created in God's image could not be the same one who invented nuclear bombs to kill others, could not be the one concocting narcotics to mess up people's minds. The man made in God's image could not be the loser walking the earth today, for God never lost a battle, his angel flushed Lucifer and his allies out of heaven for the mere thought of rebellion (Isaiah 14:12–17; Revelation 12:7–9).

Adam was a superman compared to today's

man, so what happened? There must have been a radical change, a total deviation from the prototype into the man living on earth today. A man dominated by the earth, a subdued man, who is not sure of tomorrow – that was not the picture of Adam who named all animals, shark and lion and crocodile included. Adam's rib was pliable enough to produce another human being, and yet he had no post-surgical pain, nausea or confusion; he recognised the good work right away, named her and got it right, he called her 'woman'.

Men after Adam, though the product of Fallen man, still exhibited a higher order of life than do men of the twenty-first century despite all their acclaimed knowledge. Those early men could build a tower that would reach heaven and God attested to their ability to do it (Genesis 11:6). Men like Noah could design a ship, despite not having seen one before, and yet it did not sink; he brought in all the animals in pairs. The ship was designed to house all types of animals simultaneously – a better design than the *Titanic*, despite all her builder's pride.

There was a gradual metamorphosis of natural man after the Fall from the supernatural man to the sub-natural ones we have today. When one reads the accounts of men like Methuselah, Pharez, Noah, and you see their endless lifespan, one might assume that the years were shorter, but they were not. It took a long time for the death of man's spirit after the Fall to take its full toll on his mind and body. Adam's mind was still intact after the Fall; he sewed leaves together for a dress and it fit and covered him, he was even able to hide from God. Just like switching off a car's engine when it is on a slope, it takes a while for it to stop. In like manner, it took some time for the evil impact of the fall to be fully established on earth.

One will wonder why Adam and Eve didn't quarrel or divorce; in spite of their eviction from the romantic and lovely garden they had known hitherto as home. I am sure, if it happened today, lawyers would have been hired to 'help out'. But Adam and Eve were incapable of hate. The impact of corruption on man's nature had not yet given birth to hatred. It took another generation for hatred to be imagined and hatched as seen in Cain, the son of Adam. In like manner, all kinds of evil works which exist in today's wicked world came from progressively evil imaginations born out of a corrupted inner man.

> *And God saw that the wickedness of man was great in the earth, and that every imagination of the thoughts of his heart was only evil continually.*
>
> *Genesis 6:5*

The bitter truth is that this evil will continue to worsen until Christ comes back.

This know also, that in the last days perilous times shall come. For men shall be lovers of their own selves, covetous, boasters, proud, blasphemers, disobedient to parents, unthankful, unholy, without natural affection, trucebreakers, false accusers, incontinent, fierce, despisers of those that are good, traitors, heady, high-minded, lovers of pleasures more than lovers of God.

2 Timothy 3:1–4

If the unsaved man on the street is, therefore, a metamorphosed product of the fallen man, a total deviation from God's plan, then his race, colour, advancement, education and sophistication or whatever criteria are used to categorise him are therefore of little value.

Surely men of low degree are vanity, and men of high degree are a lie: to be laid in the balance, they are altogether lighter than vanity.

Psalms 62:9

It is only a man who rediscovers the real man reborn in him who can stand the evil and truly overcome the peril of mankind's Fall, whether here on earth or in the world to come.

The Man Adam

Adam, the prototype of God's kind of man, operated as a spirit being. He was a spirit being living in a quickened body, so he was called a living soul. What we now call supernatural after the Fall is similar to the natural realm Adam lived and operated in. Adam did not need to pray to live this supernatural life. He did not need to be baptised in the Holy Ghost to operate in this realm, for he was a quickened soul, already naturally bearing the breath of God; God's breath or spirit was part and parcel of Adam's being at creation.

Adam and God

Examining the relationship between God and Adam at the beginning in the Garden of Eden, we can note the following:

(i)   Adam was God's offspring (Luke 3:38). He had the nature of God, but lived in an earth-compatible house (body), made of earthly material for true compatibility. Adam was not a man because he lived on earth; Jesus was the son of man, yet he came down from heaven (John 3:13). Adam was not a man because he had a body – angels descend with an earth-compatible body many times in the Bible, they were seen and touched, Jacob even fought with one till he blessed him, Abraham spoke to and fed angels.

Adam was a man because that was what

God called him, and it was what all creation called him at his arrival on earth – no wonder he named her that was made from his body part 'woman'. Adam had no capacity to die, for he had God's life and nature. The big question one would ask is, If Adam had God's nature, why then did he sin? Could God sin as well? This brings us to the reality that God was not God because of Adam, but Adam was Adam because of God. The first phrase of the Bible says 'In the beginning God...' So he that was in the beginning, and supreme to all, was and is still God. Adam was not God, though he had the nature of God. Eating of the fruit would not have been a sin had God not called it sin. If Adam had eaten the fruit a day or an hour before the instruction, nothing would have happened. What killed Adam was not the fruit itself. What ruined Adam and brought humanity to the doom of enmity with God was not the fruit as a molecular object; it was the disobeying of God's Word. God's Word is the source of all life on earth; moving in the opposite direction to it was a flow against the current of life.

If God had given Adam a different instruction, however ordinary the thing he chose to forbid, if Adam had disobeyed that instruction it would have had exactly the same consequence as what happened in Eden when Adam ate the fruit. The tree was the Tree of Knowledge of Good and Evil because God called it that. If he had called it any other thing it would have been just that, even if the content was the same. Things come into being because God says so.

(ii) Adam was God's companion on earth. There was a form of fellowship between God and Adam, something personal, even though He was the Most High. They had an agreement, a oneness, and so God was said to have come down in the cool of the day to see Adam. They were familiar with his coming to the extent that they knew the sound of his feet (Genesis 3:8).

(iii) Adam was God's steward on earth. The earth was and is the Lord's; the garden planted there was planted by God and for God. Man was to tend the garden and live within God's blessing for doing what he was instructed to do (Genesis 2:15). Adam named all the animals – he had access to God's mind and so whatever he called them, God called them too. If Adam had named them something God did not approve of, God would have corrected

Adam. He is a perfect God and nothing short of perfection would have being allowed (Genesis 2:19).

(iv) Adam was God's voice on earth. In naming the animals, Adam gave voice to God's idea, he voiced God's conception. Oh what a great life that was, man giving the divine idea a voice! It was a rare privilege that man in his true estate was given. Not even angels were given such privileges on earth. In the beginning, it was man's privilege. After the Fall of man, whenever an angel came on assignment to earth, what they were actually doing was giving voice to divine ideas, giving birth to these ideas in the earthly realm. God did not argue with the angels even when they were harsh. For example, Gabriel took Zacharias' voice away for a season because he questioned his voicing of the divine idea or plan (Luke 1:18–22). For the same reason, the Lord instructed David, through Gad, to quickly make a sacrifice to ask for forgiveness, so that the angel who bore God's sword of divine judgment on Israel might stop what he had been sent to voice (1 Samuel 24:15– 25). The angel of the Lord appeared to Moses and spoke as if he was God the Almighty, but he was an angel. Jacob wrestled with an angel, not with God the Father, and the angel blessed him by proclaiming him to be a prince and not a trickster any longer. When the angel of the Lord appeared to Mary, he spoke directly to her of what would happen. He did not speak like a prophet. This was Adam's privilege as a man, giving voice to divine ideas on earth and setting them in motion. So are you a spirit-being, you need to keep voicing divine ideas in order for them to find physical manifestation.

(v) Adam was God's instrument of dominion on earth. Adam subdued Eden, thereby maintaining order and ensuring absolute compliance of all creation to the divine will. Nothing argued with him, not even the devil, who had to negotiate via a medium (Genesis 1:26).

(vi) Adam was the reflection of God's glory on earth. He epitomised divine handiwork. He was covered so completely by the glory of God that he needed no other covering or clothing. The glory was so complete that shame had no place between him and his family (Genesis 2:25).

(vii) Adam was the divine seed of continuity for all creations on earth. The ability to replenish the earth was bestowed on him. God bestowed this on him, so he needed no external or extra force, nor did he need effort to be fruitful in ensuring posterity or continuity. Adam needed no manure or fertiliser to replenish the earth, yet he kept the created species, both plant and animal, in increasing abundance.

(viii) Adam was God's pride. How strange that sounds but it is true. Everything was good by God's standard, the moment it was spoken and manifested. When Adam came into the equation, God did not see another good creation, but a very good one. He was the crown and quintessence of divine spirit, crafted in blood and flesh on earth (Genesis 1:31).

(ix) Adam was the custodian of divine blessing on earth. After the process of creation was finished, there was a need for a force of progressive sustenance, a force that guaranteed a positive aura, advancement and increase, this force is called blessing. Blessing is not material, as God had created all material needs in the garden before he created Adam. Yet he still had to bless the man (Genesis 1:28–30). The blessing carried the power to reproduce, create, sustain, increase and protect the material world under the influence of Adam. That was the force or power God bestowed on Adam when the Bible said that God blessed him. It wasn't that God gave him material gifts; what God did was to give him the spiritual force to control and command the material world on earth.

Adam received God's blessing on the earth. After creation, there was a need for the earth to be sustained, subdued and replenished. God did not wish to perform this replenishment himself, time and time again, so he blessed Adam. What this means was that he put his blessing in Adam and that was all the earth needed to be sustained, replenished and dominated, or put under synchronised control so that nothing would go haywire – no tsunamis, earthquakes or volcanic eruptions, for the earth was subdued.

(x) Adam was the representative of God on earth. He was what the whole of creation saw as God, for he was made in the image and the similitude of God. I am sure if any of God's other creations had needed something from God on earth, God would have referred them to Adam. If any of them had had issue with their name, God would have sent them to Adam, for he named them in the first place.

Adam and Angels

Angels definitely came on the scene before Adam; they are spirit in totality and excel in strength (Psalm 103:20), but they were created for a different purpose. They are in a different class to man and serve a different purpose in the divine plan. Angels, like Adam, are called God's sons (Job 2:1). Satan, a fallen angel, was referred to as a son, too. We are never told that God was mindful of them or visited them. Until death came on Adam, man was above them in the hierarchy of life; man was made a little lower than angels through death (Psalms 8:4–5; Hebrews 2:6–9). Only when Jesus Christ released us from death did the order get reversed once more. Now we can boldly declare that angels are sent to cater for the man reborn in the similitude of Jesus Christ, the last Adam (Hebrews 1:14). We are no more made lower but are to be served by the angels, for we are not subject to death any more, glory to God! One thing we are sure of is that God created heaven and earth and gave earth's ownership to Adam. So if angels ventured on earth, it must have been by Adam's prompting or invitation, or to carry out assignments for Adam. This honour is now reserved for the saints! We determine how effective the angels are on earth in doing what they are sent to do on our behalf. We can weaken our angels or strengthen them (Daniel 10:11–13). We can request angelic help as well in time of need (Mathew 26:52–54).

Adam and the Devil

As we saw earlier on, the devil was Lucifer, a former angel, fallen angel or an angel of darkness. After sin was found in Lucifer, an anointed cherub (Ezekiel 28:13–15), he was sent packing from heaven, along with his lieutenants, by a host of angels led by Michael, an archangel (Revelation 12:7–9). What does this tell us? It was a demotion. The devil was demoted from his lofty position (as cherub or elder) and humiliated by an archangel, which in the angelic realm is lower than a cherub. He was thrown out of heaven and sent down, so he became the lowest of all spirit beings, along with his fallen angels, now called demons or angels of darkness in the hierarchy. If the angels were now higher, more powerful and more relevant to the divinity than Lucifer (now called the devil, diabolous) and the demons, certainly Adam was much higher. So Adam was of a higher class by all standards than the devil. The devil could not kill Adam, he had no strength, capacity or power to do so. Adam could only self-destruct. For God said, 'The day you do this, you die.' The ability to die was placed in Adam's hand by the Word of God. Unfortunately for him, he used it. No wonder the Word said that death *came by* Adam, not *on* Adam (Romans 5:12).

Adam and the Earth

Adam in his true estate was in charge of the earth. God put him in charge, which means that the ability to take charge was already inherent in Adam when God announced his lordship of the earth.

'Have dominion, replenish and subdue the earth' (Genesis 1:28). Adam had what it took for the wind not to blow contrary to him. He had what kept the sea in its place. The earth would not quake as long as Adam was in charge. There were no eruptions of any sort. Nothing could hurt on earth in the presence of Adam. The lion would not kill the goat, the crocodile was a peaceful animal, the sharks, tigers and bears were pleasant to live with because Adam had what it took to be in charge. He was a spirit-man totally in control of the earth and its contents. Weeds and thorns could not grow in the garden while Adam was there, the ground had no ability to give Adam stress. Thorns and thistles, which signified stress, hurt and hardship, only came after Adam relinquished dominion (Genesis 3:17–18).

There is no record of Adam cutting grass, using herbicides or pesticides. Weeds or tares could not manifest themselves as long as Adam was there. Some people believe that God told Adam to work in the garden, cutting grass, weeding and getting bruises all over. This is not how it was at all. How small would the garden have to have been if Adam was to be this sort of gardener – cutting, weeding, uprooting overgrown shrubs and trees, seeing the garden was well irrigated by rivers – he was just one man! That is why we have no account of him carrying a scythe or a mower, swearing, cursing and complaining. Adam's presence was the mower, it was the herbicide and the pesticide. Bacteria, viruses and fungi were all harmless to Adam's well-being. Nothing was pathological or predatory towards him, he was a man in total control.

Adam and Eve

One of the astonishing things about Adam, the spirit-man, was the way he and Eve related to each other. They did not quarrel, but had eternal oneness. Why? They had no ability or capacity to fight, disagree or quarrel, for they were like God. Even when Lucifer became the devil, there was no account of God shouting in anger and jumping up and down because one of His creations had committed mutiny. It was the angel that fought Satan and threw him out of heaven. No wonder then that when the woman brought Adam the fruit, he ate, no question or fighting!

All the above depictions of Adam from the scriptures are of the prototype man. The plan of divine creation is to enable man to be reborn as an offshoot of Jesus Christ, the last Adam, who defeated sin and death and has more glory than the first Adam and lives for evermore. You need to appreciate who you are as a spirit-being.

We have established that Adam, who was operating supernaturally in Eden, was not mere flesh and blood; he was not just a bundle of books and ideas. Adam, created in the image of God, was a spirit-being. No wonder the Bible said, *'In the image of God he created him, then male and female was the created man manifested in flesh'* (Genesis 1:27). After the fall, Adam stopped being a living soul or, essentially, a spirit-being. Spiritual death came as a result of the Fall. All human races that came after Adam, whatever their colour, were born in the similitude of he who had died spiritually. Man can only function properly and occupy his unsubdued-able, indestructible, ever-winning, ever-productive, ever-replenishing and ever-increasing status by moving from the realm of spiritual death to the realm of life. In this realm, you are not just a soul and body going about with a dead, un-regenerated spirit, but a living spirit who possesses a body and lives in a body. This is what it means to be of the spirit, but you cannot yield the peaceable fruit of life in the spirit when all you do is just nod in acknowledgement with no corresponding action. True spirituality produces God-ordained results when you consciously see yourself in the light of the spirit and live within it.

Nicodemus asked Jesus how he was so formidable and successful; he replied that the engine room was his spirit (John 3:1–8). Jesus was not sounding religious, but was emphasising the reality of his operation. As a believer born in the order of Christ, as a new man in the spirit you can only optimise the value of redemption if you will see your spirit as the engine room of divine plan and purpose. A man's whole existence as a believer is determined by how he relates to the spirit realm and how much he can get done in the natural realm of life. Your link with the realm of the spirit, where the godhead resides and operates, is your own spirit. All divine providence and potency can only be transmitted to you through your spirit. No matter how much power is available in Christ, no matter how much light is available in him, no matter how much victory he has won for you, you can only make these things relevant in your earthly life if you lay hold of them in and through your spirit.

For this reason, I will be using the remaining part of this book to show you what potent spirit forces are already made available to you through new birth. You can never lose or fail if you live your life in the flesh with an overwhelming consciousness of, and deliberate operation within these potent spiritual forces. Jesus, our ultimate example, operated within them and left us to follow in his footsteps.

Chapter Three

Well Able your Ability to Know

This chapter will deal with the inherent ability in your spirit made available by knowledge, to succeed in all life's battles. It is not just potent; it is a must-have for your triumph as a believer. When we talk of knowledge, we are not talking of intellectual knowledge (gnosis) here. We are not talking of that which comes by mere intellectual engagement.

When God said, 'My people are destroyed for lack of knowledge', he did not mean the lack of a college degree; as good and desirable as a college degree is, he meant that they lacked the appropriate kind of knowledge. What is the appropriate kind of knowledge? Knowing the things of God. What are the things of God? The things of the spirit, because God is a spirit (John 4:24).

The force we are going to see here, therefore, is that which is potent in man's spirit through appropriate knowledge. Many words can be used to describe the word 'ability'. Among these words are 'power', 'strength', 'energy', 'intensity' and 'might'. By implication, all these words, even in the world of science, describe force at work. The common denominator of all of these words used in describing force is the fact that they can be possessed, used to exert influence, to get things done or effect change when the need arises.

Talking of the ability of the spirit, we mean the power, strength, energy, intensity and might resident in a believer's inner man or spirit which must be consciously possessed and used to exert positive influence within and without, to get things done and effect positive change in their life and the lives of others. We are not talking about the Holy Spirit here, we are talking about *your* human spirit. It does not matter how powerful, mighty, strong and intense the Holy Spirit is as a personality, He cannot work or get things done in you outside the vehicle of your spirit-man. That is why God woke your spirit-man up through salvation before sending the Holy Ghost into you. So when we talk of using all the ability or the force of the spirit to effect positive change, we are talking of the inherent ability of your own spirit-man made alive by redemption and then kept alive by the presence of the Holy Spirit in you.

Any time you need to influence things in and around your life, you need not to look elsewhere; you need to look within first and engage the ability and might within you. Any time you want to get things done in your career, in your home, in your body, in your finances, all you need to do is look inward first. The ability to effect a change in your life lies not with the doctors, even though they will try their best in diagnosing, prescribing or even operating on you. But, friend, you need to know that, as good as all these are, they still do not guarantee recovery, and many still die daily in spite of increasing scientific advancements. The ability to effect the change you desire lies not with local politicians in your area, nor does it lie with the fellow next door, in the office or even in your clan; the ability lies within you. It is time to stop and engage the ability within you, as a spirit-man, to effect that change, exert that influence and get those good things done.

Wherefore I desire that ye faint not at my tribulations for you, which is your glory. For this cause I bow my knees unto the Father of our Lord Jesus Christ, of whom the whole family in heaven and earth is named, that he would grant you, according to the riches of his glory, to be strengthened with might by his Spirit in the inner man; that Christ may dwell in your hearts by faith; that ye, being rooted and grounded in love, may be able to comprehend with all saints what is the breadth, and length, and depth, and height; and to know the love of Christ, which passes knowledge, that ye might be filled with all the fullness of God.

Ephesians 3:13–19

The above scripture is a picture of the kind of prayer believers should pray for themselves and for others; but alas, how different it is from the superficial prayers you hear all over the place, even from many pulpits. Here we see the Apostle praying for the force of the spirit to be operational in the believers' lives at Ephesus. 'Strengthened with might.' What a phrase! Both words allude to the force of the spirit. Why would Paul the Apostle be praying such a prayer in a time of difficulty or tribulation for a people, when it looked like all things around them were crumbling and giving way, when confidence was ebbing and boldness seemed to wane (Ephesians 3:13). He prayed such a prayer so that they would not faint. Why? Because if they do not faint, they will get glory or victory out of what they are going through (vs. 13b), meaning that what they are going through will eventually bring them glory. You can see he did not say 'which will bring God glory.' Of course, God is glorified when His children are winning, breaking forth on all sides and rubbing the nose of the adversary on the floor. God is not so insecure not to glorify His own people. All glories belong to God, but there is a certain dimension of glory he has reserved for His own, which He crowns them with perpetually (John 17:2–5).

Friends, when things seem difficult, hard and

very challenging, you need not faint; it is not the time to throw in the towel or start accepting defeat as your fate; it is not godly to just sit down and accept defeat. No, no way. You are meant to conquer the tribulation, for it is ordained for your glory. This means that when you are sick, you are meant to be healed and receive glory in the healing grace of your Lord and Master, Jesus Christ. When your bank account seems low, you are meant to conquer poverty and eventually glory in the abundance that will attend your way. Nothing is strong enough or bad enough to take you down and keep you down. All things are meant to work together for your good.

And we know that all things work together for good to them that love God, to them who are the called according to his purpose.

Romans 8:28

This is to say that good and not bad is expected as the result of all life's conflicts. The truth is that whether or not this is your tangible experience, it is still the reality of God's purpose concerning you. The truth which is the sanctifying Word of God is truer than all of mankind's experiences and excuses put together. I would rather, therefore, line up with the truth than hang my head, drop my shoulders down and wallow in pity and defeat.

There is no place for a pity party in your life, no matter who is planning to attend. I am not just a motivational speaker; I am a preacher of the gospel of Jesus Christ, which is the power of God unto salvation. So I am not trying to excite you, I am making you see who and what you are.

In Ephesians 3:16, the Apostle described the only solution to life's crises and battles. He prayed for this solution on behalf of the believers in Ephesus and I believe in it, for you, too. The solution is to engage the strength, might or ability of your regenerated spirit. How much of it I am willing and able to engage determines how much I win. The blame game, bitterness and frustration will not solve serious problems, only my engagement of the right forces will. Engaging the force made available to us in God who is a Spirit (John 4:24) is what guarantees lasting victory full of glory, which is our calling. We are called to show the opposition what stuff we are made of: the very good, never losing, ever conquering stuff of Jehovah, glory to God!

Our anchor verses for this chapter (Ephesians 3:13–16) were born out of the preceding verses. So verses 10–19 can be partly summarised as: God ordained you to torment your troubles, destroy your adversaries, overcome the opposition and turn the mountain. He did not call you to run away from challenges or to despair in fear and timidity, but to engage your challenges with the strength within, the might in your spirit and win, thereby basking in the glory of the overcomer you truly are.

One of the many reasons I love God's Word is because it does not leave us in limbo as to what to do in any of life's situations. When folks say things to imply that God's Word (the Bible) is ambiguous, contradictory, complicated, merely philosophical, confusing or incomplete, the illuminated ones just wonder what they are talking about. This is because God's Word is not just complete, it is tried and tested. It has been proven over and over to help men who engage it in the right way to deal with life's situations, including the issue of eternity (which no mortal can run from, no matter who they are, whether they believe in it or not). When men cannot get enough light to deal with life's darkness from God's Word, it is either because they are not saved (Mark 4:11) or because they have a wrong, irreverent, sloppy, indifferent or closed minded approach to the Word. If, according to Ephesians 3:10–16, God wants you to trouble your trouble and conquer all opposing forces through engaging the forces He releases into your spirit, somewhere within this divine prescription must be outlined how to use this divine elixir. Verse 16 is not the end of the prayer, verses 17–19 are.

That Christ may dwell in your hearts by faith; that ye, being rooted and grounded in love, may be able to comprehend with all saints what is the breadth, and length, and depth, and height; and to know the love of Christ, which passes knowledge, that ye might be filled with all the fullness of God.

Ephesians 3:17–19

Having been born again, the essence of Christ, the Anointed One, living in you can only be realised through faith. This makes the subject of faith of the utmost importance for Christians. It is not a denominational doctrine; it is not meant for a specific group or movement, as many want us to believe. It is the main subject and the main issue of Christianity. No wonder a man can only be called a Christian after exercising faith in the saving grace of our Lord Jesus. I will now leave this topic for other chapters and other books to deal with more extensively.

When you are born again, you have responded to God's love and you need to bask in it and grow in His love, discover it the more. The platform of God's relationship with mankind is love and love alone (John 3:16). All God's purpose, all His promises and all His provision for the emancipation and glorification of mankind are based on love. No wonder the Psalmist echoed the voice of an inquirer in Psalms 8:4: *'What is man that thou art mindful of him? Or son of man that thou visitest him?'* Whether you are up or down, God has his mind full of you. No matter your qualification or lack of them, tribe, race or background, God's mind is full of thoughts about you, and good thoughts for that matter (Jeremiah 29:11). Many people think it is only when things are going right in their lives – food on the table, money in the bank, a car in the garage, health in their body, husband or wife by their sides, a baby in the cot, and so on – that God loves them or that they can be sure He does. But love is God's personality, not just something he is trying to do. He cannot love less, even while we were sinners he loved us. That is why John 3:16 says **'God so loved the world.'** He so *loved.*

Therefore, we can say God loves everybody equally and this is absolutely true. He loves drunkards, addicts and extremely sinful men. But the difference between the saints and the sinners is their response to God's love... 'That whosoever believes in Him'. Who is this 'Him'? He is the evident manifestation of God's love, 'Jesus Christ'. Even within the household of faith, the extent of your response to God's love will dictate your ability to receive consecration, victory and blessings. It will decide how far you walk with God in obedience and receive his provisions and promises.

Believers' triumph in life is rooted in the love the Father (God) has for us.

Nay, in all these things we are more than conquerors through him that loved us.

Romans 8:37

For He has made us a joint heir with His son Jesus, underneath whom he has subjected all things, be it humans, demons, spiritual, material or immaterial things. Thank God you are one body with Christ. You are sitting with Him in heavenly places in God, far above all things (Ephesians 2:1–6). The basic response to God's love is faith... *'Whosoever believes'* (John 3:16b). Faith is what brings Christ, who is the expression of God's love, into our hearts (Ephesians 3:17a). You are expected to explore this love and maximise what is on offer. Earlier I called this the root of believers' triumph in all life's issues. You need to get to the very depth, height, width and length of it, for that is where you will find triumph. All the victory you long for is hidden therein. If all the strength and might you need to engage your spirit-man and stay on top of the mountain of life, and not in the valley of despair and failure, are pack-aged in God's love through Christ Jesus, there must be a way to access it. Friend, the access is "knowing":

...that you may be able to comprehend.

Ephesians 3:18a

...and to know.

Ephesians 3:19

Therefore how much force (might and strength) of the inner man I am able to engage in life's issues, how much triumph I see, whether I cave in, give up or faint is not a matter of how tough the issue is or how wicked the devil is. It is a matter of how much I comprehend and how much I know. How much I comprehend, know and engage is what determines how much of God's energy will be operational in me to deal with life's issues.

So we have learnt that God loves everyone equally and promised to provide equally for everyone in Christ. The Bible shows us that the level at which God is at work in each one of us depends on our own investment in knowing, comprehending and engaging Him and His love in our lives. This will even consequently have a bearing on the level of divine response and intervention we get or enjoy when we pray.

Now unto him that is able to do exceeding abundantly above all that we ask or think, according to the power that worketh in us.

Ephesians 3:20

So it is not enough to be religious and keep making God look like a wicked, uncaring and unresponsive monarch. It is better to understand the workings of the King's kingdom.

If knowing is a potent force, we need to know *how* to know and *what* to know. God is a spirit (John 4:24), the one who had seen Him before said so. If God is a spirit, the knowing that will engage God or God's purpose, promises and provision has to be rooted in the spirit as well.

No wonder intellectual acumen and academic attainments, as good as they are, cannot reveal God to any man. No wonder many of them try in futility and pride to comprehend God, whether in the laboratory or library, but cannot. When all their wrongly motivated and wrongly directed efforts fail, they come to the shallow conclusion that God does not exist. But, thank God, He does exist. He speaks to us, lives in us and we shall see Him face to face one day!

When a man is born again, his spirit-man comes alive. This is the real man; it is the very part of man that has the capacity to comprehend God or know the things of God, and hence the knowing ability is spirit ability.

For what man knoweth the things of a man, save the spirit of man which is in him? Even so the things of God knoweth no man, but the Spirit of God. Now we have received, not the spirit of the world, but the spirit which is of God; that we might know the things that are freely given to us of God. Which things also we speak, not in the words which man's wisdom teacheth, but which the Holy Ghost teacheth; comparing spiritual things with spiritual. But the natural man receiveth not the things of the Spirit of God: for they are foolishness unto him: neither can he know them, because they are spiritually discerned. But he that is spiritual judgeth all things, yet he himself is judged of no man. For who hath known the mind of the Lord, that he may instruct him? But we have the mind of Christ.

1 Corinthians 2:11–16

In concluding this chapter, the message is thus: when challenges obstruct your way, do not faint or give up. These challenges are meant to yield glory as you engage the knowledge of God's love to confront them. This knowledge will release strength into your inner man, with which to overcome mountainous troubles, escape valleys of despair and glory in the victory Christ has already won for you. Challenges are like veils and behind them is glory. If you summon enough strength to remove the veil, you will see the glory (Ephesians 3:13–16).

Chapter Four

The Light Within

When at the beginning of the previous chapter I said the knowledge we are talking about is not merely intellectual, it was not to sound verbose or to condemn academic acumen and excellence, it is just that the knowledge of God is of a higher order.

Considering the thick darkness that envelops the Fallen Man's world, with its attending challenges, the ultimate solution is that man needs light. The light of the spirit is made available to you by God in three components; these components will deliver into your hand the victory that the Lord won for you. You cannot consistently engage in these components and miss out on victory, it is impossible. All the glorious victories resident in the length, breadth, height and depth of God's love, accessible through knowing, can only be attained through these components. I will therefore be showing you the power of the components; illumination, direction and discretion. The illumination, through your spirit, of your mind puts you at an advantage; it puts your mind far above darkness, for the light shines in darkness and the darkness cannot stop or comprehend it. Light exposes you to the impact of your divine provisions and inheritance in Christ Jesus. It makes the resurrection power that raised Christ from the dead functional in you (Ephesians 1:18– 20). When you understand and follow divine direction, your welfare, safety and status are automatically placed in the hand of the one whose kingdom you are representing and living in. Living illuminated and knowing the right direction to take in life helps you make sound decisions, taking the right actions at the right time. Goodness and mercy will have no choice but to follow you.

I will now dissect these powerful components with you as individual entities.

Illumination

The first component is divine illumination, which is a vital aspect of God's provision for you to triumph over darkness in life. It is so distressing seeing believers living in the utter darkness of confusion, depression and frustration. It is improper to see a man with a regenerated spirit trapped in a corner, not knowing what to do, where to go, what to lay hold of or even how to. It is not normal. Jesus always knew what to do at the end of the day and he always hit the target – not by trial and error, but by definite illumination of His spirit from on high. How much glory you are able to get out of darkness depends on how much illumination you are able to access through your spirit-man. Oh, how many battles believers have lost by groping in darkness, marrying in darkness, doing business in darkness! When driving in the dark, the speed of your car, the model or the colour is not what determines your safety, but how much illumination you are able to gather. Many avoidable accidents in the life journeys of believers are primarily due to lack of illumination. It is so easy to start running like a blind horse, but darkness can only be removed by light. Before you start running helter-skelter, you need to know that this age is one of gross darkness.

Arise; shine; for your light has come! And the glory of the Lord is risen upon you. For behold, the darkness shall cover the earth, and deep darkness the people; but the Lord will arise over you, and His glory will be seen upon you.

Isaiah 60:1–2

Whenever there is an issue of darkness at hand, no matter how gross the darkness, light is always the solution. Whenever God wants you to arise, that is to be on top of the situation, light is the solution, 'arise for your light is come'. Whenever God wants to show the glory of the triumph of Christ Jesus in you, light is what He gives... 'For your light is come.' So the first thing God wants to do for a believer is to illuminate him, then he can raise him. The reason there are many casualties in various aspects of our lives is because many are saved but not illuminated. Many prefer to go for 'special deliverance' than to get illuminated.

There is a saying in my tribe that 'the lazy man ends up doing the hardest or the most difficult of all jobs'. This is also true in the things of the spirit. When you see the look, body language and unspoken reaction on many people's faces when the teaching is getting long or deep in many church assemblies, you will know where their priorities lie. But if you promise them a quick fix, especially if they won't have to do anything, learn anything or take any responsibility, you will see people sitting up and giving their full attention. But God does not operate like that; true glory comes by divine illumination.

Ask any number of sons and daughters of Zion who attend meetings and give offerings how many Christian messages they listen to or how many faith-building books they read in their personal time. Ask them how much personal study they do with intensity – not drowsily when they are about to go to sleep after watching late-night TV. When you ask this, you will see why personal victory generally seems far-fetched. A man cannot do more in God's kingdom than he is illuminated to do. He cannot reach beyond his own light. This is why it is so important to pay attention to the level of illumination you have achieved in the kingdom.

God's Word is light (Psalm 119:105). Jesus said that the Word, among every other prescription, is the ultimate and sure elixir for triumph in life. Extolling Mary's choice of the illumination that comes through the Word, Jesus told the very caring Martha that as good as caring and catering is, Mary's choice was still the wise choice. In fact, the master said that of all the parts at hand, the good part was what Mary had chosen. It took her away from the losers' camp. When what you have is taken away from you, it is often said that you have lost it; so Jesus said Mary was immune to losing in life, what she had could not be taken from her no matter how hard the enemy tried.

Now it happened as they went that He entered a certain village; and a certain woman named Martha welcomed Him into her house. And she had a sister called Mary, who also sat at Jesus's feet and heard His word. But Martha was distracted with much serving, and she approached Him and said, 'Lord, do you not care that my sister has left me to serve alone? Therefore tell her to help me.' And Jesus answered and said to her, 'Martha, Martha, you are worried and troubled about many things. But one thing is needed, and Mary has chosen that good part, which will not be taken away from her.

Luke 10:38–42

When you are born again, you are actually born of the Word.

1 Peter 1:23

The Word is light, no wonder you are called the child of light.

1 Thessalonians 5:5

Now when Jesus had heard that John was cast into prison, he departed into Galilee; and leaving Nazareth, he came and dwelt in Capernaum, which is upon the sea coast, in the borders of Zebulon and Nephthalim: that it might be ful-filled which was spoken by Esaias the prophet, saying, The land of Zebulon, and the land of Nephthalim, by the way of the sea, beyond Jordan, Galilee of the Gentiles; the people which sat in darkness saw great light; and to them which sat in the region and shadow of death light is sprung up.

Matthew 4:12–16

The above scripture clearly shows Jesus's mission and his mode of accomplishing it before His public ministry began. Even the region and shadow of death is fixed by illumination. No issue can be too dreadful or threatening to your well-being that light cannot handle it successfully. We know Jesus is the true deliverer, he has unlimited ability to deliver us, but He does it by light, as we can see here. True and lasting deliverance comes by light. If you invest half the effort you use to seek a quick fix in achieving illumination and lay hold of that light in confronting the challenges you are facing, you will realise how easy it is to claim the victory which has already been purchased on your behalf by Christ. You will not only win, you will master winning.

When you are born again, you move from the domain where darkness rules into the very domain of light (Colossians 1:12). Darkness then has no right over you. Vitally, it is your responsibility to make light real. The deal is done on your behalf, which is why you are admonished to walk as an illuminated child of God, which you are legally (I Thessalonians 5:5). If as a believer you are born of God or have your source from God as a spirit-being, and God is light, we can then conclude that your spirit takes its source from light. Your spirit therefore has no compatibility with darkness by nature. Confusion, depression and subjugation by darkness have no place in your make-up. Your inner man has the inherent capacity to respond to and make use of the light of divine illumination, no matter what you are going through on the outside. That is where your true freedom lies.

The light here is not optical light, but the true light which is the source of life and essence of God. It is the majestic glory of God the Father. God, the true light, gave optical light to all the physical light-manifesting bodies – the sun, stars and all energy sources harnessed by scientists to give optical illumination in any form.

The real you, which is the inner man, is born again of the incorruptible Word of God and that Word is light. So your inner man ought to be an illuminated personality. No wonder Jesus made an audacious statement like, *'I am the light of the World'* (John 9:5). While Jesus was here, he unapologetically called himself the light, he even called you, his follower, light as well (Matthew 5:14). You should therefore see it as an insult for a believer to be harassed by darkness or oppressed by darkness. It is equally demeaning to live in darkness, just jumping here and there looking for what is not lost and yet making no headway. We need to examine certain issues concerning illumination.

(i)   *'Let your loins be girded about, and your lights burning'* (Luke 12:35).

One of the things I find interesting about Jesus, whenever I read the account of His earthly life and ministry, is the profoundness and the audacity with which

He passed messages across. Here we see Jesus saying simply and clearly that the amount of illumination you enjoy, the intensity of the burning you enjoy, is your responsibility... 'let your'. Jesus was saying that if, at any time in your life, the equilibrium appears to be shifting against you on the side of darkness, all you need to do is allow the light in you to burn. Girding your loins means sitting up and getting your spirit fixed. Like a lamp that's not burning well, get it trimmed and burning.

(ii) *'When the unclean spirit is gone out of a man, he walketh through dry places, seeking rest; and finding none, he saith, I will return unto my house whence I came out. And when he cometh, he findeth it swept and garnished. Then goeth he, and taketh to him seven other spirits more wicked than himself; and they enter in, and dwell there: and the last state of that man is worse than the first'*
(Luke 11:25–27).

This shows you who is in the driver's seat when it comes to your freedom: you are. The amount of freedom you enjoy is not the responsibility of he who cast out the devil, nor is it the responsibility of the devil cast. The devil is just looking for a place to live, the emptiness or fullness of the house is the determining factor. This is the responsibility of the landlord – you. No one can be illuminated on your behalf, no matter how much you mean to them. Wake up! May I say here that revelation and vision, both crucial to Christian development and fulfilment of divine destiny are both products of illumination. Jesus said that which reveals or exposes any hid-den thing is light. This is the illumination we have been talking about. This shows that you cannot access the revelation of divine truth unless you are illuminated within. Your vision can never be clearer than your level of illumination within.

The good news is that your spirit-man contains the God-given ability to be illuminated. Your spirit is a lit candle; fan the light to brightness and walk in light. When you were saved, you were saved into a family, the family of God. In this family are inheritances meant for you to walk in and live on while on earth to obtain a heavenly experience. God knows you need these inheritances and cannot do without them if you are to run a resourceful and successful race. You don't need to make any special application to be part of this inheritance. When you were saved, you obtained it automatically (Ephesians 1:10–11).

Obtaining the inheritance is not necessarily the same as enjoying the inheritance. For example, you can be invited to a dinner, totally paid for, in very posh place. You can be provided with an outfit and even chauffeur driven there. Food and drinks can be on the table and everybody can be having a nice time. Having obtained an invitation to the dinner, your admittance is not an issue, but partaking in the goodies is another matter. It is possible to attend such a dinner and still be starving. No one can do the eating and drinking on your behalf, even if they attend the dinner as your aide. How long you have been saved, how many people met you in faith and your position in the assembly are irrelevant when it comes to the enjoyment of your inheritance.

(iii) *'Giving thanks unto the Father, which hath made us meet to be partakers of the inheritance of the saints in light'* (Colossians 1:12).

Illumination is the platform from which you can partake or participate in this inheritance, which you qualified for by new birth. This warranted the Apostle

Paul's prayer for Ephesians' Church, lest they miss their inheritance and start blaming God. *'The eyes of your understanding being enlightened; that ye may know what is the hope of his calling, and what the riches of the glory of his inheritance in the saints'* (Ephesians 1:18).

It means that the extent of their enlightenment is the extent to which they will be enriched with the glory of their inheritance, which belong to them as much as to the saints.

(iv) *'The spirit of man is the candle of the Lord, searching all the inward parts of the belly'* (Proverbs 20:27).

Your inner man or spirit is the candle, lit by new birth. Set it on a candlestick, let it give light to the whole house or your whole life. As beautifully and wonderfully made as your body is, with all the senses seemingly sharp and accurate, it is just a house; it cannot give you light, no matter which school you send it to or what train-ing you give it. This shows how demeaning it is for believers to be running around for astrological prediction to their destinies or direction in life. Lay hold of light within. If you are tired of groping in darkness, put your spirit in its right position in the hierarchy of life and you will enjoy the unlimited ability and benefits of divine light in all life's issues.

Direction

One of the greatest tragedies of this age is lack of direction, even among the saints, and it ought not to be so. Families, business, corporations, institutions and nations run aground daily because of leaders who have little or no regard for direction. God does not want His children to gamble with their lives; 'maybe, maybe not' should not dominate the issues of your life. People think it is a form of humility to be unsure of what to do and how to do it in our life as believers. You hear people saying words like, 'Only God knows', even though in their hearts all they mean is that the will of God on the matter is out of reach and mysteriously hidden for ever and all we can do is grope around.

There are occasions in life when you are not sure of the details of the steps you are taking, even though you are surely being led by God. The truth is that even when you lack the details, he will not deny you the immediate direction. Your spiritual leaders are there to guide and help you in building your faith; the secular leaders set the direction for an orderly society; parental guidance provides the training needed in your journey into adulthood.

But God himself is the director of your paths. Friend, God has not and will not leave the map-ping out of your life in anybody else's hands. Leaders and parents are like schoolteachers set on your path by God as signposts to guide you while you are evolving. God's ultimate plan is for you to lay hold of divine direction and walk without stumbling in all areas of your life as you grow up in Him. God has a good and glorious plan for your life, but not every road you see will lead there. Some roads may look good, easy to navigate or even familiar but hear this: *'There is a way which seemeth right unto a man, but the ends thereof are the ways of death'* (Proverbs 14:12; 16:25). Such a road does not look rough, dangerous or seem wrong. The coordinates and parameters seem right, past experience assures it to be right, but alas it is not just wrong, the end is full of calamities. The Bible called it 'a way' at the beginning, but towards the end it becomes 'the ways' of death, which signifies multiple or compound calamities which are out of control. Many casualties people suffer in life as a result of taking the wrong road to their desired destination start off as a good way, but end up as multiple confusions. Many finances, marriages, careers, health issues and lives are in ruins or fighting unnecessary battles today as a direct result of making a wrong move, taking a wrong turn, initiating and sustaining a wrong association or moving in the wrong direction. The gospel truth is that most, if not all, of them are avoidable, especially now that you are saved; I therefore see a way out for you today, in Jesus's mighty name. Amen.

> *Blessed be the God and Father of our Lord Jesus Christ, who hath blessed us with all spiritual blessings in heavenly places in Christ.*
>
> *Ephesians 1:3*

On what platform is direction accessible to you as a believer?

(i) **Direction is in the promises of God for his people.**

God is a spirit; His promises and provisions exist only in the spirit realm. Though you live in the earthly realm, your citizenship is of the spirit world where Christ is seated; you have to reach out into that realm to lay hold of them.

> *Thus saith the Lord, in an acceptable time have I heard thee, and in a day of salvation have I helped thee: and I will preserve thee, and give thee for a covenant of the people, to establish the earth, to cause to inherit the desolate heritages; that thou mayest say to the prisoners, go forth; to them that are in darkness, shew your-*

selves. They shall feed in the ways, and their pastures shall be in all high places. They shall not hunger nor thirst; neither shall the heat nor sun smite them: for he that hath mercy on them shall lead them, even by the springs of water shall he guide them.

Isaiah 49:10

God is saying that the only guarantee He has for His people against hunger, thirst and all that smites them is that He will lead them. Though He heard them in accept-able time, which means that prayer will command a divine audience in an accept-able time, it will never replace being led. There are many inheritances that are still lying desolate and God wants His people to inherit them, but the platform is in being led. People are busy praying, but God is saying, 'I have heard, now I want to lead.'

Not all believers will be pastors, not all will be preachers, not all will be business-men or women and not all will be entrepreneurs, but God still wants all to inherit the desolate places, but they can only be led by him into such a lofty inheritance. The things which eyes have not seen, which ears have not heard, which are not yet revealed to men can only come to you by being led. It is impossible to do great exploits as a Christian in any endeavour without harnessing divine direction. The good news is, this direction has been promised to you.

(ii) **Direction is a privilege of God's people.**

> *For the Lord's portion is his people; Jacob is the lot of his inheritance; He found him in a desert land, and in the waste howling wilderness; He led him about, He instructed him, He kept him as the apple of his eye. As an eagle stirreth up her nest, fluttereth over her young, spreadeth abroad her wings, taketh them, berate them on her wings: so the Lord alone did lead him, and there was no strange god with him. He made him ride on the high places of the earth, that he might eat the increase of the fields; and he made him to suck honey out of the rock, and oil out of the flinty rock; butter of kine, and milk of sheep, with fat of lambs, and rams of the breed of Bashan, and goats, with the fat of kidneys of wheat; and thou didst drink the pure blood of the grape.*

> *Deuteronomy 32:9–14*

However dry or deserted your initial position in life is, it does not matter to God. All you need is to be led and you will soon be swimming in butter and milk with honey, which signifies supernatural abundance, pleasure, ease and sweetness. God cannot pick up his people from the desert and still leave them dry, broken, busted and famished. God is the one who picks you up in distress and leads you by the side of still water until your soul is restored and replenished; he then plants you in a green pasture for timely flourishing and fruitfulness.

The twelfth verse of the above scripture leaves sole responsibility of leading you to God, 'So the Lord alone did lead him', you are not allowed to play a game here. He alone knows where the butter and milk are, and he can differentiate the poison from the food. When he leads, he also protects you from wickedness and uses all His might and care to protect you as the apple of his own eye. No matter how careless a person is, when it comes to watching after his own eyes he will do it with certain degree of diligence. Now God said, 'As long as I am the one leading, you are the apple of my eye and I will not watch you being hurt.' God is the most high; his leading can only end you up in high places in life. You can't be led by God and miss your season of lifting!

(iii) *Direction is part of divine provision.*

> *But God led the people about, through the way of the wilderness of the Red sea: and the children of Israel went up harnessed out of the land of Egypt. And Moses took the bones of Joseph with him: for he had straitly sworn the children of Israel, saying, 'God will surely visit you; and ye shall carry up my bones away hence with you.' And they took their journey from Succoth, and encamped in Etham, in the edge of the wilderness. And the Lord went before them by day in a pillar of a cloud, to lead them the way; and by night in a pillar of fire, to give them light; to go by day and night: He took not away the pillar of the cloud by day, nor the pillar of fire by night, from before the people.*

> *Exodus 13:18–22*

The above scripture gives the picture even before the Red Sea was parted, before He healed the water of Marah or gave the manna, which shows how much it mattered to God to lead His people, much more than the miracles and the material provisions. God would rather lead you than give you material things, because if he is not there and Pharaoh pursues you hard, you will lose the materials. So the first provision God made for them in their journey of destiny was divine leading. Why did God not lead them by the cloud both night and day? Because He wanted them to have clarity in His leading. God will have you move from the realm of not being sure to the realm of certainty and clarity in following divine leadings. The last verse said he took not away the provision of leading, the pillars of cloud and fire. No matter what you go through, do not forsake divine leading. Direction will save you from taking a wrong step even when you face challenges. If you ignore direction, you will complicate the trouble.

(iv) *Family menu.*

> *For as many as are led by the Spirit of God, they are the sons of God.*
>
> *Romans 8:12*

Divine leading is part of the family menu, a provision for the sons of God, which you are as a spirit, male or female. You can only access divine direction through your regenerated spirit. You need to have the utmost regard for spiritual signals before seeking or following God can start yielding the peaceable fruits that go along with it. Your priorities in life will determine what you pay utmost attention to: if your priority is to be the very best God has ordained you to be and to have what he wants you to have, then you need to consciously reach out for the ability of your spirit-man to harness the right direction by divine leading, and walk therein.

(v) ***Custodian of divine plan.***

God is the architect and master-builder of your life. While you, as His labourer, are putting the bricks together here on earth, you need to really be in touch with Him and be sure you are building what He designed for you. Remember, He told Moses to build according to the pattern he was shown. What if Moses had chosen to do otherwise? Thinking God did not go to the Egyptian schools of science, he went (Acts 7:22). What if Moses had altered the pattern because it didn't appeal to his mental, psychological or emotional frame? What if Moses did not see what was being shown to him in the first place? God would have disapproved of him because he would have built a wrong house (Hebrews 8:5). All He designed for you is good, perfect and pleasant (Jeremiah 29:11). All that God has got in stock for you to build is good and pleasant, even if it initially makes little sense to you or to the people around you. It is your life, your God; therefore take responsibility to know. When you know, you can boldly follow.

> *For I know the thoughts that I think toward you, saith the Lord, thoughts of peace, and not of evil, to give you an expected end. Then shall ye call upon me, and ye shall go and pray unto me, and I will hearken unto you. And ye shall seek me, and find me, when ye shall search for me with all your heart.*
>
> *Jeremiah 29:11–13*

Discretion

The ability to make the right decision is vested in your regenerated spirit-man. Your spirit-man is not limited to optical vision so he sees what you cannot see. When God sent Samuel to Jesse's house to anoint him a king, Samuel, by the judgment of his mind based on what his optical eye communicated to his brain, hailed the wrong man as the chosen one and God had to intervene to put things right. We talked about the importance of the right choice earlier on, and the peril of getting it wrong, but at the end of the day, our choices are based on our discretions or judgments. God expects you to mature in the things of the spirit. He doesn't want you making the wrong choice or taking a wrong turn so that he has to intervene all the time; for this reason He has equipped your spirit-man with the ability to take the right decisions based on good judgment or discretion.

But solid food is for the mature, who by constant use have trained themselves to distinguish good from evil.

Hebrews 5:14

As simple as this passage sounds, life and death depend on it – many graves are filled with victims of a lack of discretion; many divorce papers are written with the ink of a lack of discretion; many careers are ruined on the platform of indiscretion – you won't be a victim in Jesus's mighty name. When God left, the devil visited Adam's household. Adam had what it would have taken to know the subtleties of the devil, but he did not impart this knowledge to Eve and, for whatever reason, Eve did not see the serpent as an adversary. The devil did not come into the garden as a fiery or venomous snake, as people think. The serpent or snake we know today is a product of the fall in Eden. It appeared as a nice-talking, subtle creature. All the might in hell could not have taken Adam and his family down, as they were blessed. That was why Satan did not bother using strength or might with Adam – all he deployed was wiles and they fell for it. Eve's conversation with the serpent had no tone of struggle or argument, it was a conversation rooted on a pedestal of familiarity and presented with what sounded like genuine interest for the welfare of Adam's family, but alas it was a trap; no wonder we were not admonished against the power but the wiles of the devil (Ephesians 6:11). Even the darts of the wicked one are rooted in wiles (Ephesians 6:16). The devil is said to roar like a lion, which means he is not one but pretending to be one (1 Peter 5:8).

It was a different ballgame when same Satan came tempting Jesus at the onset of his ministry. Jesus's victory hinged on seeing and recognising Satan as an adversary. He saw him and addressed him as such, no matter what Satan offered him. Mind you, we are not told that Satan came with two horns on his head, as you see in comic books. He did not even come with superpowers, fighting and struggling with Jesus and with Jesus hurriedly calling for reinforcements from the angelic. He came as a good fellow, sounding as if he had Jesus's well-being at heart, trying to proffer a solution for his immediate needs and offering a fixed deposit in his account for future needs. He came promising heaven and earth; but, thank God, Jesus had discretion at work in his spirit. He recognised Satan as an adversary offering temptations, so his victory was inevitable. When you walk in discretion, you will not fall victim to evil or succumb to unproductive, destiny-destroying relationships; you will judge all things and yet not be judged.

> *A good man sheweth favour, and lendeth: he will guide his affairs with discretion. Surely he shall not be moved for ever: the righteous shall be in everlasting remembrance.*
>
> *Psalms 112:5*

As a believer, you ought to reach inward and guard your life with discretion. You cannot afford to go along with the trend when making your decisions in life. Discretion is the ability to judge all things with divine perspective and put them in their right place, so you do not fall victim to the wicked one. This makes your place in destiny secure. You will be immovable, no matter what is going on around you or how angry your adversaries are.

You may wonder why God did not tell Adam about the devil and the possibility of him coming so that Adam could prepare. God knew what Adam had within him as a spirit-man made in the image of light (God). He knew Adam had the capacity to discern darkness. That was why God judged him, even though Adam tried to make up excuses. God said unto Adam, *'Because thou hast hearkened unto the voice of thy wife'* (Genesis 3:17). The unspoken part of that statement would have been 'In spite of all you have within you and know!'

God does not expect you to live in suspicion, going about looking for demons in every place or everything and everybody; but if Satan uses natural methods to manipulate issues round you, discretion enables you to make the right decision, take a stand and shine with light. Consider the following:

(i) *JUDGMENT*

Discretion will help you to judge what God has judged, embrace what He embraces, and permit what He permits. You will not even negotiate for what God will not buy. As a believer, if you consciously follow the discretion in your spirit-man, you will not sin and even if you do sin, you will judge yourself and repent to obtain forgiveness, thereby escaping divine judgment.

> *But if we judged ourselves, we would not come under judgment. When we are judged by the Lord, we are being disciplined so that we will not be condemned with the world.*
>
> *1 Corinthians 11:32–33*

(ii) *PRESERVATIVE*

Discretion puts you squarely in God's camp. If God is for you, who or what can be against you? Many wars would be ended if we all walked in this vital ability resident in our spirit.

When wisdom entereth into thine heart, and knowledge is pleasant unto thy soul; discretion shall preserve thee, understanding shall keep thee: to deliver thee from the way of the evil man, from the man that speaketh froward things; who leave the paths of uprightness, to walk in the ways of darkness; who rejoice to do evil, and delight in the frowardness of the wicked; whose ways are crooked, and they froward in their paths: to deliver thee from the strange woman, even from the stranger which flattereth with her words; which forsaketh the guide of her youth, and for-getteth the covenant of her God. For her house inclineth unto death, and her paths unto the dead. None that go unto her return again, neither take they hold of the paths of life. That thou mayest walk in the way of good men, and keep the paths of the righteous.

Proverbs 2:10–20

Exercise

Discretion as an ability is resident in your regenerated spirit. Keep exercising your limited mind to lay hold of light in your spirit, unlimited to judging things. Not leaving things to mere sensual feelings is the secret of development and coming of full age spoken of in Hebrews 5:14. When doing physical exercise, people start from some-where, no matter how low, and gradually keep engaging their physique in the desired exercise until it becomes part and parcel of them and starts yielding unto them the desired results. Discretional exercise works in the same way. As you master a class, you get promoted. I see your promotion come in torrents, culminating in you being lifted, through right judgement in Jesus's name. Amen.

Finally in this chapter I would like you to appreciate the fact that resident in your spirit is the knowing ability of illumination, direction and discretion. This gives me joy when I meditate on it because I know darkness, in whatever form it comes, is helpless against you. You have the ability, so use it, friend. Stop being confused, perplexed and dazed. He that comes from above is above all things and so are you. Nothing is strong enough to daze you.

Chapter Five

Power from Within

> *In the last day, that great day of the feast, Jesus stood and cried, saying, 'If any man thirst, let him come unto me, and drink. He that believeth on me, as the scripture hath said, out of his belly shall flow rivers of living water.' (But this spake he of the Spirit, which they that believe on him should receive: for the Holy Ghost was not yet given; because that Jesus was not yet glorified.)*
>
> *John 7:37–39*

Jesus here makes a profound statement of what will become of those who believe in him after his glorification. He makes us realise that power will be resident within us – so much that it will flow out. Religion teaches us to always look up for everything, especially when it comes to spiritual ability, but the master himself here says this is wrong. There are times we should look inside ourselves to release the flow of what He has deposited in us already. Jesus knew that religious men could display false humility. He knew they might not want to hear this message, so he waited until the last and great day, then He stood and cried. Our hearing and understanding of the issue was of such utmost importance to Him that He could not whisper it or send someone to echo it. He cried 'Out of your belly is resident a river source.' Jesus was not just talking about pastors and preachers; he meant all that believe in him and he knew what he was talking about. He knew a time would come when issues around us would warrant us reaching out for the help of his spirit, a time when all we learnt at college would not be sufficient to see us through and place us above life's challenges, a time when all we have learnt is not enough to prepare us for all we are confronted with. You are not expected to lift up your hands and cave in to trouble. Your victory was bought, sealed, signed and stamped when Christ died, was buried, rose up and ascended to glory.

Out of your Belly

Jesus did not say that the rivers of living water would flow from heaven, but out of the believer's belly. The belly will determine the flow, friend. How much your belly is able to let out will determine how much flows for you. The flowing force depends on the belly, not on any obstacle in the way of the river. Many rivers are dried up, broken into streams or made stagnant by an obstacle in the way of their flow, but the outcome has nothing to do with the path of flow but the source. Every believer is rooted in Christ (John 15:5), Jesus cannot change (Hebrews 13:5); He is a constant for ever, so the only variable in this equation is the belly. How much progress you make in life is a belly issue!

Jesus did not say the flow would come from heaven. Why? Because when you were born again, your spirit came back to life. When the Holy Ghost comes inside you, he takes up permanent residence and lives within your spirit. The Holy Spirit is the Father living within us. He is the spirit that made Jesus Christ (the Anointed One). He is the source and fountain of the living water; your belly or spirit is the reservoir. Out of you ought to flow the rivers of living water, not just a river of tongues. Your belly is where heaven lives on earth; the very innermost being of a Christian is where God lives. Many are dry, with no river flowing from them, even though they have been Christians for ages. Some are even pastors, ministers, deacons and some may have a PhD in theology, but still be dry, depressed, oppressed and full of fear. This is because it is a belly issue and not an issue of post and position. Jesus said 'Out of the belly of *whosoever believes*', not 'whosoever has position, degrees or title'. The river can only flow from the innermost core of a Christian person, but religion can make people superficial and believe otherwise. Thus they can remain dry.

In a bid to be humble, people look to heaven for the river. No, Jesus said, it is in the belly of believers. Many would like us to believe it is the privilege of a few to experience this river, but Jesus said, 'He that believeth.' No wonder many pastors look and sound buoyant, they have experienced buoyancy, but their congregations are a bunch of dry, depressed, oppressed people, looking for water in all the wrong places; they have been made to believe the river is just pulpit-based. Jesus said it ought not to be so, *'he that believeth out of his belly shall flow rivers of the living water.'* (John 7:38.) Your spirit is the belly; make it available as a reservoir for the divine water of life. Even though we ought to look up to heaven in order to receive, most of the time our answers are routed through our belly (spirit) where the Holy Spirit serves as our connection to heaven. Jesus said that the Holy Spirit will receive of him (from heaven) and show to us (on earth)... (John 16:12–14).

Shall Flow

Thank God Jesus did not call what you have a lake! Thank God He did not say, 'out your belly shall come stagnant pools.' He said, 'Shall flow'. It is a forward-moving river. Your progress and unlimited forward movement in life is dependent on the flow. A deep belly with great water capacity will produce great river, with great volume and capacity for movement and use. Such a river cannot be stopped; even if you dam it, you will have to let it go soon or else it will swell, burst and breach the dam with a devastating effect. When the well within you is full and the river starts bursting forth, you become unstoppable no matter what opposition you are confronted with. You might go down, but can never be kept down. When the opposition reinforces and seems insurmountable, fill up within for a flowing forth without; you will breach all the barriers in front of you.

A believer, therefore, can only be held down for only a short while, can only be hindered for a short while. When water starts flowing from the deep belly, a breach will occur, a bursting forth, with devastating effect on the boundaries. Nothing is strong enough to hinder you unless you choose not to flow or move forward. Rivers do not flow backwards; therefore a believer should not have a backward mentality. Never have the mind-set of someone who can be stopped or disadvantaged; a flowing river has only one mind-set, which is to go forward no matter what.

I have heard Christians talk of great ideas in terms of their career or business. While I am about rejoicing in the spirit that they are catching on, you hear stuff like, 'But the problem is capital' or 'But I have some limitations in terms of so-and-so.' You start wondering why a stagnant pond is coming out of them instead of a flow of living water. 'Oh, I am just being realistic,' they say. No, you are not being realistic, you are destroying your river of possibility, you are diminishing the possible momentum, you are stopping the river, you are flowing backwards.

So, what do I need to do? Start a positive confession? I have tried this many times, but it does not work, they say. As a Christian, you do not need a positive confession because you should not have a negative one in the first place. You are admonished in Philippians 4:8 to fill your mind with good and positive things. When you are full of such things, out of the abundance of your heart your mouth will speak. In all situations, fill your belly with what you want from God's Word. Meditate and seek fellowship with the Lord so that an anointed river will start flowing. You shall see mountains reduced to chaff. Do not let tradition and religion hinder the flow of your river. Go forward, make progress, conquer more lands and expand your horizons.

Jesus had such a buoyant inner-man that He could not be stopped by any force, human or demonic. He needed no one to pity or encourage Him to take on his divinely assigned destiny on earth; not even a personal bereavement could stop him.

John the Baptist was he who was leaping in the womb when Jesus came on the scene; he introduced Jesus to his first disciples and boldly declared him to be the Lamb of God (Luke 1:39– 41, John 1:29).

It was John who ushered Jesus into his anointing through baptism and yet John's head was given to a damsel as a prize for a dancing competition. Many may question why Jesus did not do anything to help John if He was all He claimed to be. Some would not only question the master's authority, but his family loyalty, since John was His cousin. Coupled with the bereavement, Jesus faced these accusations, yet he was neither broken nor frustrated. Herod was an absolute ruler, so John's family could not press any charge against the murder. Yet Jesus continued going about doing good and remained strong. No wonder Nicodemus came for some lessons at night, even though it was dark and risky.

Rivers

Blessed is the man who does not walk in the counsel of the wicked or stand in the way of sinners or sit in the seat of mockers. But his delight is in the law of the Lord, and on his law he meditates day and night. He is like a tree planted by streams of water, which yields its fruit in season and whose leaf does not wither. Whatever he does prosper.

Psalms 1:1–3

A river, in the natural sense, causes things planted along its course to flourish, prosper, and be fruitful. As a believer, you are not looking for prosperity; nor are you looking for coolness and calmness from coast to coast. Resident inside of you is that which makes for prosperity and will bring calm and coolness to you in the heat of life's challenge. Out of your belly flow rivers; it is high time you looked inwards. If you pay maximum attention to your belly (spirit), and if the spirit (belly) is well built like an ever-increasing fountain, an ever-expanding and jealously guarded well of infinite capacity, then no blessing will be unattainable nor will any fruit be too much for you to bear. When the river is full of water, the river bed is the first beneficiary. You are not the river but it flows out of your belly, hence all that concerns you is situated by the river bed and is therefore the first and main beneficiary of what flows from within before it flows forth. The river should water your health, career, finances, family and everything that concerns you.

In natural life, rivers are landmarks; the size determines the significance and use. Many nations are shaped by river boundaries and will do all it takes to defend such a river and keep it flowing. In nature, the volume of water in a river is what determines the force with which the river flows, what resistance it can overcome, what it can sweep away and how far it can go in its course. In like manner, the volume of living water at work in your belly (spirit) determines the force with which it flows in your life; it determines what level of resistance you can handle, what can stop you, your boundaries and limitations. In fact, the river size determines how useful you can be to God. For example, in natural life you cannot use a stream for hydroelectricity, not even for large-scale irrigation purposes. Why? The force generated by streams is too little for such a task.

When, as a Christian, you start praying for God to use you, bless you and make you a blessing to humanity, the Lord says that using you is not a problem, just work on your belly (spirit), enlarge the capacity therein to take more water and you will start generating enough force to irrigate others, to irrigate nations and generate light for nations. Can we then conclude that even divine security has a lot to do with this? A strong nation will do everything possible to possess and protect her great rivers, another nation cannot just come and dam or possess it. This means a believer's security depends on man's inner capacity. What kills others will spare you, what possesses many cannot even come near you. Why? Belly capacity. Heaven will do anything to defend and protect her treasured gem and that is what you are. The water put into a river, by rain or other methods is the determining factor of the river's volume and thus the water output. In like manner, the belly output of a believer is a product of the belly's input by divine connection. How much living water gets into the belly (spirit) of a believer is what deter-mines how much water goes out of the belly. Your river size, strength, force or capacity cannot go beyond the amount of divine substance you feed on by the water of the Word and fellowship of the spirit. How then do I fill my rivers?

The Rain of the Spirit

The presence of the Holy Ghost is likened to the pouring of rain upon our spirit. We can also see the apostles being filled again and again by fellowship with the Holy Ghost (Hosea 6:3, Zechariah 10:1, Acts 4:31). After the baptism of the Holy Ghost, which is a once-and-for-all event, you must keep experiencing being filled with the Holy Ghost consistently. This comes by fellowship. The apostles in the above scripture did not ask to be filled or for a double portion of anything; they only fellowshipped with the Father by way of prayer and were refilled with divine presence, which manifested within them. Prayer was not a programme or doctrine, but a fellowship. As you seek fellowship with God in the spirit, the river starts getting swollen or refilled within you, until you cannot contain it again but must let it flow forth.

Water of the Word

> *Husbands, love your wives, even as Christ also loved the church, and gave himself for it; that he might sanctify and cleanse it with the washing of water by the word.*
>
> *Ephesians 5:25–26*

We are being shown here that God's Word is water; therefore the more Word you have in your spirit (belly), the greater the water capacity within. When you invest your time and other resources in enlarging your Word capacity, you are increasing your water capacity for rivers of living water manifestation.

> *It is the spirit that quickeneth; the flesh profiteth nothing: the words that I speak unto you, they are spirit, and they are life.*
>
> *John 6:63*

The profitable Word is the spirit-Word. Bible reading must then be spirit-enhanced and spirit-focused, which means reading, listening to messages and reading of books should be with the mind-set of receiving something into your spirit by the enabling power of the Holy Spirit. A receiving attitude is the prerequisite for belly infilling needed for belly outflow. Many people read the Bible to argue, some for quiz competitions, many listen to messages in the service merely because the sermon is an item on the programme. What a wrong attitude? Whenever you are interacting with God's Word, in any form or place, it should be with a belly- or spirit-capacity-expanding attitude, a receiving attitude, an attitude of a hungry and thirsty person who wants to be filled, no matter your present level of fulfilment.

Many would rather dance, shout and jump in church, which is not bad, but when it comes to the Word they are bored, looking at their watches. No wonder they are dry and afraid when alone. Many only pray in the spirit in church to show that they are still born of the spirit. Many have been saying the same thing for ten years with no depth, no intimacy with the Holy Ghost. Being too proud or busy to listen to messages or read books is a short cut to limiting your belly's capacity. Priority has to be given to that which builds and expands the inner man's capacity, for that is the belly from which rivers will flow. The water you refuse to put in can never flow out, God cannot be mocked. A believer's belly or spirit ought to be filled, both in and out of season, because out of a filled belly should flow rivers; not only when you are in church or among believers, not only when things are going right in your life. Jesus said, *'Out of your belly or your inside shall flow the force to effect the change you need in the outside.'* (John 7:38.)

Living Water

The water within you is living not stagnant, stale or dead. Watch what you bring forth in words, actions and even your unspoken body language. Your words should make things go up and not down, strengthen you and not weaken you, make you see the way forward and all possibilities. Your words should make you the vantage one and not the unfortunate, helpless loser.

> *For the Lamb which is in the midst of the throne shall feed them, and shall lead them unto living fountains of waters: and God shall wipe away all tears from their eyes.*
>
> *Revelation 7:17*

We can see here what the water does: it is for wiping away tears from the eyes of the redeemed. Friend, I can see your days of mourning ending. Jesus said, *'Out of your belly shall flow that which terminate tears and wipe sorrow even the living waters.'* (John 7:38.) You need stop crying and look inward for an outflow of grace. God acts on the platform of the waters. He has waited long for you to let grace out and let Him work on your behalf.

> *Now when I had returned, behold, at the bank of the river were very many trees on the one side and on the other. Then said he unto me, These waters issue out toward the east country, and go down into the desert, and go into the sea: which being brought forth into the sea, the waters shall be healed. And it shall come to pass, that everything that liveth, which moveth, whithersoever the rivers shall come, shall live: and there shall be a very great multitude of fish, because these waters shall come thither: for they shall be healed; and everything shall live whither the river cometh.'*
>
> *Ezekiel 47:7–9*

The capacity of the living water to turn things around is painted clearly in the above scripture; the water is presented as a catalyst for fruitfulness, which is not just about being productive now but also in securing the future. Similarly, the blessed man in Psalms 1:3 is likened to a tree whose future is wrapped in the fruits it produces. Even when the tree stops existing, another of its kind will spring up for posterity and perpetuation of blessing. I therefore curse barrenness to its root in your life now, in the mighty name of Jesus Christ. Amen.

As a believer, you are fruitful, a person with a future or, even better, you are the future. We live in a world and at a time full of gloom and doom. Evil, depressing and hopeless news is broadcast everywhere, but there is a river of hope in you as believer. Whatever the water in you touches shall live. The water, as we have seen, must start flowing from within your spirit, so the fruit can start appearing on your table, in your body, at your office, in your bank account, in your marriage, in your children and in all that pertains to you where you direct the river. Seasonal fruits are a product of seasonal watering; an abundance of fruits are product of much watering. When you start seeing the fruit depends on when you start the watering – your season is of your own doing. When a man is waiting on nothing, he gets nothing. When a man is planting nothing, watering nothing and doing nothing but going about singing 'It's my season', frustration born out of delusion and self-deceit is inevitable. When you are up and doing, filling you belly with the right stuff, leave the mockers, just let it flow forth from within you in words and actions. You will soon be the man of all seasons and all season will soon be for you. When the water flows out of you in words and actions your leaf shall not wither; the outward effect of inward investment shall not be lacking. That which is sweet around you will not die; that which is living will not die.

Growing up as believers, we were erroneously made to believe that a spiritual man is one who is sullen, gloomy and uncertain, someone who is not sure of tomorrow, just hanging on a thread of grace. But this is not true by any means; as a man of the spirit, you are always buoyant, with an infilling and outflowing belly full of vitality and divine colour, like a tree planted by a river, always abounding in grace.

It is abnormal to watch things wither away around you. People often use their mouths to turn off the tap of the river of living water, meant to cause the withering to disappear. It is a pity seeing saints justifying failure, sickness, divorce and all kinds of withering. People make God's Word conform to their situation instead of doing other-wise. A farmer might not be able to stop a drought from coming, but he can water his farm so that his plants will not die, in spite of the drought, but rather flourish and produce. That was what Isaac did in time of drought – he dug until water came forth to water that which he had sown and his plants flourished. No wonder the neighbours envied him! (Genesis 26:1a; Genesis 26:19–21; Genesis 26:12–13, 22b; Genesis 26:14).

So, instead of looking for pity, blackmailing people around you with negative emotions, dig deep inside, bring forth the rivers of living water from your belly and keep watering that which is withering, it will soon be green. Whatever you do, as long as the river is kept flowing shall prosper; you will see progress, improvement and success. When you allow the influence of the rivers of water from your spirit to act on your natural endeavours or career, there must be an out-standing result – the kind the ungodly cannot have… *'The ungodly are not so'* (Psalms 1:4–5).

When you engage the force of the river from within, watering all issues with the water of the Word by the spirit, nothing can stop you from progress, irrespective of your age, sex or location. You will become in-suppressible, no opposition at work is strong enough to stop you, the river from within will sweep away all hindrances and stumbling blocks. If it looks like the opposition is increasing and the failure or the sickness is gaining the upper hand, keep on digging inside, let the river keep flowing outward, you will soon have a flood to sweep them away.

Remember the story of Noah – it had to rain for forty days but in the end the water prevailed. God did not stop pouring forth the water until He saw His desire upon His enemy fulfilled (Genesis 7:17–24).

Many saints do not wait for the water they are bringing forth from within to turn into a prevailing flood before they stop the rain; many give up too easily after pouring ten, twenty, a hundred or a thousand buckets and there seems to be no outward sign of a change. Now that you know better, I see a change on its way for you.

Stop sighing and complaining, for you belong to a winning breed. You will get your desired result, no matter how long it takes or how many reservoirs you have to empty. What matters is that you prevail over the issue at hand, making progress and moving forward as you have been called, ordained and destined to.

I see your star rising now.

Conclusion

The Unstoppable You

Let all men be liars and God be true. Jesus was called the true and faithful witness, which places his report about you above all your experiences, past or present. His report surpasses that of your adversaries and everyone around you. What did he say?

> *Do not marvel that I said to you, 'You must be born again.' The wind blows where it wishes, and you hear the sound of it, but cannot tell where it comes from and where it goes. So is everyone who is born of the Spirit.*
>
> *John 3:7–8 (NKJV)*

What a word from the Master's mouth! Jesus said that a man born of the spirit can be likened to a wind that does as it pleases. A man who is born of the spirit, as we saw earlier, is essentially a spirit living in a body – he is moving, acting as a spirit, so he goes where he wishes. I love this statement, '...He goes where he wishes' – not where his background wishes not where his geographical location wishes, not where his degree wishes, nor where his race or skin colour wishes. He goes where he wants to and nothing can stop him, he has no limitations. He cannot see any, so cannot entertain any. When the river is really swollen, the river beds give way. The limitations on the left and on the right, which are placed there by nature, cannot stop a flood. If there are boundaries I can't conquer, the reason is me, not the boundaries, because all I need is a strong and turbulent flow and all limitations will fall away.

Many people are living other people's dreams and lives, so no fulfilment, or breaking forth or contentment is achieved. Jesus said, 'Your movement in life should be on the pedestal of what you wish.' This is why the Word admonishes you to have your mind renewed so that you will wish what God wishes for you.

And be not conformed to this world: but be ye transformed by the renewing of your mind, that ye may prove what is that good and acceptable and perfect will of God.

Romans 12:2

When you have this mind-set, you start moving like the wind; public opinion will count less with you. Many destinies are sinking because the owner is out to impress people. As a believer, the power of light puts you in the knowledge of God's will.

When this divine will becomes your wish and you start moving on its impulse, you become an unstoppable force. Not only will you make progress, your profit will soon appear for all doubters and mockers to see.

Jesus said that even though the operation of the wind might not be understood, the impact is undeniable; it is the same for you, man of the spirit. You might be misunderstood and called names by sceptics, but your impact will soon hit them in the face and the sound of your victory will not be hidden from them, in Jesus's name.

Jesus said, the wind does not ask permission to blow, nor does it wait for a conducive environment, it blows anyway. You are a blowing being, a forward-moving, unstoppable one; as a believer you are not meant to be a quiet, easy-going loser. If your blowing will ruffle feathers, you might as well go ahead. God is far more interested in your forward movement than your gentlemanly nature.

Jesus said, the Kingdom of God suffers violence and only the violent press hard to lay hold of it. If Jesus behaved as a gentleman with the devil, or with the Pharisees and the Sadducees in the spirit of meekness, He probably would have been robbed of his destiny. He knew the nature of the opposition He had to deal with, so He was ready to blow forward like a whirlwind; He wasn't prepared to blow where, how and when they wanted him to, but where He himself wanted to, how he wanted to and when he so desired.

Towards the end of Jesus's ministry, He said He beheld Satan fall like lightning. If at falling the enemy was still fierce like lightning, it shows us how determined he was to stop Jesus's destiny; but thank God for Christ, he was more fierce in getting to his destination. He had in store much more than the enemy could invest into stopping him. Friend, how far and how soon you are ready to give in to any opposition is what determines if he could stop you. Resident in your spirit is the unstoppable ability to go ahead, to go far and be accomplished.

Finally, I pray that you will not give in to the weakness in your past and background; nor will you give in to the fierceness, resistance and strength of your opposition. I pray that you will reach inward and lay hold of the omnipotence of God resident in your spirit by reason of your oneness with Christ in the spirit.

I pray you will look your mountain in the eye and tell it how incapable it is to stop you.

I pray you will say to giants that, though your outward appearance might look frail, yet resident in you is the greater one who energises your spirit for conquering all the way.

See you on top!

www.ingramcontent.com/pod-product-compliance
Lightning Source LLC
Chambersburg PA
CBHW071817020426
42331CB00007B/1514